Cumbria Libraries

3 8003 04469 3125

KU-615-290

D1467742

This book is on loan from
Library Services for Schools
www.cumbria.gov.uk/
libraries/schoolslibserv

Cumbria
County Council

LIBRARY SERVICES FOR SCHOOLS	
38003044693125	
Bertrams	26/03/2013
363.23	£12.99
LSS	

armed services

Adam Sutherland

cover stories

First published in 2012 by Wayland

Copyright © Wayland 2012

Wayland
Hachette Children's Books
338 Euston Road
London NW1 3BH

Wayland Australia
Level 17/207 Kent Street
Sydney NSW 2000

All rights reserved

Concept by Joyce Bentley

Commissioned by Debbie Foy and
Rasha Elsaeed

Produced for Wayland by Calcium
Designer: Paul Myerscough
Editor: Sarah Eason

British Library Cataloguing in Publication Data

Armed services. — (Police and combat)(Radar)
   1. Police—Special weapons and tactics
   units—Juvenile literature.
   I. Series
   363.2'32-dc22

ISBN: 978 0 7502 6443 3

Every effort has been made to clear copyright.
Should there be any inadvertent omission,
please apply to the publisher for rectification.

Printed in China

Wayland is a division of Hachette Children's
Books, an Hachette UK company.

www.hachette.co.uk

Acknowledgements: Alamy: Newsphoto 14–15;
Flickr: MashleyMorgan 20–21; iStockphoto:
MTMCOINS 1; Alex Kehoe: 26t; Royal Navy:
22–23, 2tl, 11t, 31r, 27c; Shutterstock:
Zagibalov Aleksandr 3br, 28–29, Daniel Alvarez
30b, Gary Blakeley 8l, Hung Chung Chih
24b, Danilo Ducak 27r, Homeros 9r, Andrii
Kravchenko 2tr, 9l, Stephen Meese 27l, Byron
W.Moore 19l, Regien Paassen 18t, Losevsky
Pavel 24–25, Laurin Rinder 2br, 13, Studio 37
cover, Tatonka back cover, Oleg Zabielin 6–7,
29b; U.S. Army: 10–11, 2bl, 4–5, 24t, 16–17,
16; Wikipedia: U.S. Armed Forces 8r.

The website addresses (URLs) included in this book were
valid at the time of going to press. However, because of
the nature of the internet, it is possible that some addresses
may have changed, or sites may have changed or
closed down since publication. While the author and
Publisher regret any inconvenience this may cause the
readers, no responsibility for any such changes can be
accepted by either the author or the Publisher.

the**people**

the**machines**

the**moves**

the**talk**

INTO ACTION!

I stood on guard duty last night for two hours, squinting through a night-sight. Just had time to grab an hour's sleep, but now it has begun. Everyone is on red alert. This is what we have been working towards for months, right back to basic training. Before dawn breaks, the Chinooks and Apache helicopters are standing by, ready to take us deep behind enemy lines.

INTO THE UNKNOWN

We sit side by side on the choppers. The deafening rattle of equipment and thrum of the rotor blades cut through the air. Conversation is useless. We try to talk but it's easier to use hand signals – gestures we learned in basic training and respond to automatically. My throat is as dry as a desert; nerves or excitement, I'm not sure which. I'm ready to go. I want to go. I just don't know what to expect. A firefight or a complete surrender? There's no way of knowing until we get there.

COMBAT READY

It's time for take-off. The adrenalin surges through my body like a jet stream and my pulse starts to race. What will we see when we land? Whatever it is, we have to be ready for it. We're landing outside a rebel-held stronghold. We're not doing this quietly, so everyone will hear us coming. We're in the air for 20 minutes. When we land, the training kicks in. Our bodies do what they need to do and our brains barely register the danger. It's amazing what you can teach yourself.

BEHIND ENEMY LINES

We're down. The doors open, the noise of the rotors gets louder and almost unbearable. It's mixed with the shouts of the commanding officers, and the heavy thud of hundreds of boots hitting the ground running. It's my turn now. Wish me luck. I might need it.

THE FORCES

The armed services are the military forces of each nation. They can be sent anywhere in the world – sometimes to fight, but often to stop conflicts between other countries and groups. Armed services operate in different environments. Each service has its own ranks, its own special duties and skills, and its own uniforms and equipment.

ON LAND

The army is a land-based military force. Since the end of World War II (1939–1945), the size of the world's armies has shrunk dramatically as equipment and training have both improved. For example, the USA currently has 1.58 million people in its armed services, but during World War II, it had a massive 11 million recruits.

AT SEA

Naval officers on ships, submarines and navy aircraft patrol the world's oceans and defend their countries from attack. Navy vessels are often sent to areas of conflict to support a nation's army, and to provide floating headquarters for fellow armed services.

IN THE AIR

The air force uses fighter planes, helicopters and other aircraft to fight enemies, bomb targets on the ground and transport troops to battle zones. The air force also helps to keep the peace by patrolling trouble spots and can deliver life-saving supplies, or help to get people out of danger zones!

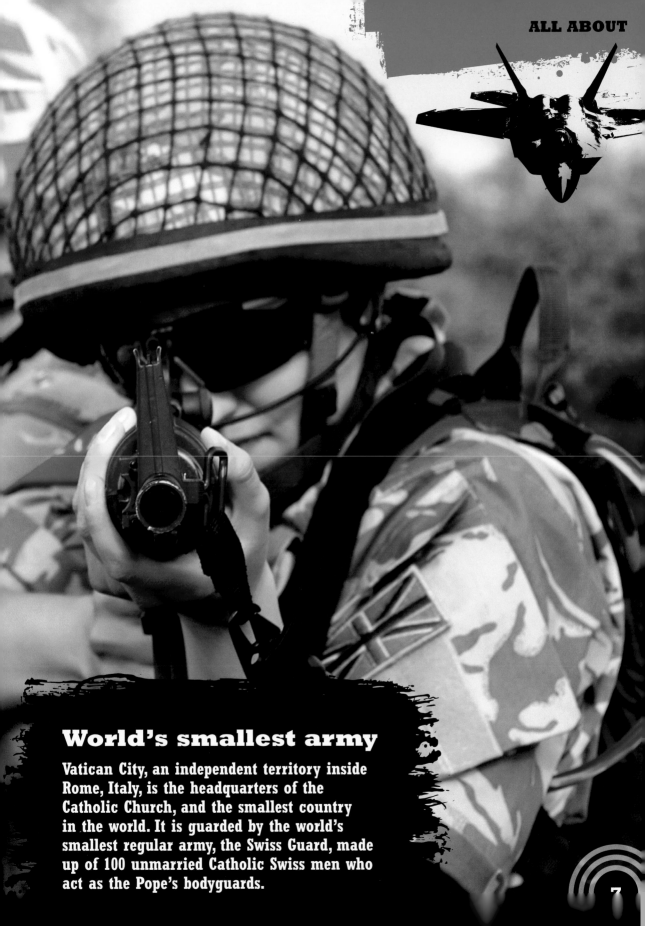

World's smallest army

Vatican City, an independent territory inside Rome, Italy, is the headquarters of the Catholic Church, and the smallest country in the world. It is guarded by the world's smallest regular army, the Swiss Guard, made up of 100 unmarried Catholic Swiss men who act as the Pope's bodyguards.

GLOBAL CONFLICTS

Wars happen when one country invades another, or when two countries disagree about each other's actions or beliefs. With more sophisticated weapons, modern wars may be shorter, but keeping the peace can be just as difficult as winning a war.

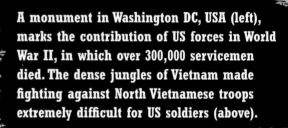

A monument in Washington DC, USA (left), marks the contribution of US forces in World War II, in which over 300,000 servicemen died. The dense jungles of Vietnam made fighting against North Vietnamese troops extremely difficult for US soldiers (above).

THE WORLD AT WAR

With more than 100 million soldiers involved, World War II was the largest war in history. It was fought between the Allies (mainly the USA, UK and Russia) and the Axis (Germany, Japan and Italy). It began in September 1939 when Germany, led by Adolf Hitler, invaded Poland. It ended with Germany's surrender in May 1945. World War II saw the USA and Russia emerge as the world's two main 'superpowers'. At the same time, European countries started to join together in the United Nations and the European Union to try to avoid dreadful conflicts like World War II in the future.

AGGRESSION IN ASIA

The Vietnam War lasted from 1955 to 1975. It was a conflict between the communist North (supported by Russia) and the anti-communist South (supported by the USA) at a time when the USA and Russia were worried about each other's growing control over other countries.

Over 10,000 air force operations were carried out within the first ten days of Operation Desert Storm (below). A multinational force worked side by side in Iraq during the invasion of 2003 (right).

The war spread to surrounding countries, with Laos and Cambodia both heavily bombed by US aircraft. The war ended when North Vietnam captured the South's capital city, Saigon. The two countries were reunified the following year.

FIGHTING IN THE GULF

When Iraq invaded Kuwait in August 1990, countries such as the UK, USA, Saudi Arabia and Egypt formed a coalition to force Iraqi troops out. Operation Desert Storm, as it was known, began with the aerial bombing of Iraqi forces in January 1991, followed by a ground assault the next month. Iraqi troops retreated just 100 hours after the ground campaign began, and Kuwait was liberated.

ATTACK IN IRAQ

In March 2003, a multinational force led by the USA and UK invaded Iraq. The Allies believed that the Iraqi president, Saddam Hussein, was building illegal nuclear weapons in his country. He was also suspected of funding terrorism. Saddam was captured, and eventually executed by the new Iraqi government. Western forces are still in Iraq – including 46,000 US troops – but full withdrawal of troops is planned by 2015.

A BRITISH SOLDIER ON LIFE IN AFGHANISTAN
MAJOR RUSSELL LEWIS

FRIDAY JUNE 10, 2011

5.30am The sun's up but it's still cool. A few of us head to the improvised 'gym' – some free weights and a dirt running track – for 30 minutes of exercise. After that, it's into the solar-powered shower. This is basically a hosepipe, but the water is warm-ish, and there's plenty of it because we have our own well. We shave every day, too – army rules!

7am Breakfast is served. We have our own cook house and all meals are prepared in the camp. Every two or three weeks, helicopters bring in fresh supplies of eggs, bread and breakfast cereal. Once that's disappeared, we're back onto tinned rations. Breakfast is porridge or a fried breakfast out of tins – beans, powdered egg and tinned sausages.

8am–12pm I'm the camp's commanding officer, so I spend my morning planning patrols, sending reports back to base, and walking around the camp, talking to the men and checking on morale. Our tour of duty lasts for six months. I have a lot of young soldiers under my command, some as young as 18, so everyone needs looking after.

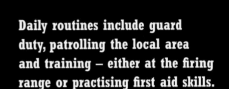

Daily routines include guard duty, patrolling the local area and training – either at the firing range or practising first aid skills.

12pm Lunch time. During the summer months, the temperature rises to 45–50°C, so after eating, the men head to their bunks with a book to escape the heat and to recharge their batteries. When you're out on patrol, engaging with the enemy, carrying a 40 kg bag on your back, it's mentally and physically exhausting. You need to rest!

5pm Dinner time. We eat with our friends in small groups – usually dishes such as pasta bake, shepherd's pie, stew or curry. These are all simple dishes that can easily be cooked with tinned rations.

6pm I get my 20 commanders together to review the day, and make plans for tomorrow. We discuss administration issues such as which parts of the camp need tidying up, or more serious stuff such as a firefight with the enemy.

7pm It's getting dark now, and the men head for their bunks. We watch films on mini DVD players, or read by torchlight. We go to sleep early as we're up at 5.30am tomorrow to do it all again!

COMBAT AIRCRAFT

The world's air forces fly the latest aircraft into battle. Here are some of the fastest, most expensive and best-equipped aircraft in the world. Take a look to see how they compare.

C-130J-30 SUPER HERCULES

Long-range transporter plane used by the UK's Royal Air Force (RAF), US Air Force and others

Wingspan:	40.38 m
Length:	34.37 m
Cruising speed:	660 kph
Ceiling:	8,534 m
Crew:	3
Cost:	£37 million

EF2000 EUROFIGHTER TYPHOON

European-designed fighter used by the UK, Germany, Italy, Spain and Austria

Wingspan:	10.95 m
Length:	15.96 m
Cruising speed:	1,315 kph
Ceiling:	18,290 m
Crew:	1
Cost:	£77 million

F-35 LIGHTNING II

Specially designed European fighter with stealth capacity

Wingspan:	10.65 m
Length:	15.37 m
Cruising speed:	1,931 kph
Ceiling:	18,288 m
Crew:	1
Cost:	£80 million

F/A-18E/F SUPER HORNET

Supersonic fighter-bomber in service by the US Navy, Air Force and Marine Corps

Wingspan: 13.7 m	
Length: 18.4 m	
Cruising speed: 1,250 kph	
Ceiling: 15,240 m	
Crew: 1/2	
Cost: £33 million	

TORNADO GR4

Fighter plane used by the RAF, Germany and Italy

Wingspan: 13.91 m (maximum)	
Length: 16.72 m	
Cruising speed: 1,593 kph	
Ceiling: 15,240 m	
Crew: 2	
Cost: £30 million	

F/A-22 RAPTOR

The next-generation fighter of the US Air Force

Wingspan: 13.6 m	
Length: 18.9 m	
Cruising speed: 1,600 kph	
Ceiling: 18,000 m	
Crew: 1	
Cost: £90 million	

KEY
m = metres
kph = kilometres per hour
ceiling = maximum flying height

HRH PRINCE HARRY

HARRY WALES

THE STATS

Name: Henry Charles Albert David Mountbatten-Windsor

Born: 15 September 1984

Place of birth: London, UK

Job: Apache helicopter pilot, Army Air Corps

MILITARY TRAINING

Prince Harry began his army career in 2005 when he joined Sandhurst Military Academy in Surrey, UK. Sandhurst is the British Army's officer training centre. To win a place at Sandhurst, 20-year-old Harry had to pass a four-day assessment based on fitness and military planning. Officer Cadet Wales, as he was known, successfully completed the 44-week training.

SECRET SERVICE!

At the start of 2007, the British Ministry of Defence (MoD) announced that Harry would travel with his regiment to the front line in Iraq. The plans were changed that summer when it was decided that Harry was a 'high value' target, and would be in additional danger from attack, which could affect the safety of his regiment. However, in February 2008, the MoD confirmed that Harry had been serving in Afghanistan for more than two months. For security reasons, his presence had been kept top secret.

TOP RANK

Harry was then given the rank of second lieutenant and joined the Household Cavalry's Blues and Royals regiment. After that he went to The Armour Centre in Dorset, UK, where he embarked on a course to become an Armoured Reconnaissance Troop Leader.

FLYING SKILLS

In January 2008, Harry began training as a pilot with the Army Air Corps. In March 2011, he qualified as an Apache attack helicopter pilot. Only the most talented pilots in the army are given the chance to fly Apaches, which are valued at £35 million (US$57 million) each. In April 2011, Harry was promoted to the rank of captain and could return to Afghanistan for a combat mission as early as 2012.

RANK AND FILE

The US Army has its own ranks and responsibilities. Services are divided into three groups: enlisted people who join at the lowest ranks, the non-commissioned officers or NCOs (usually enlisted men or women who have been promoted to more senior positions) and commissioned officers, who are in the most senior positions of authority.

GENERAL

A general usually has over 30 years' military experience and is the senior level of commissioned officer.

COMMISSIONED

COLONEL

The colonel commands brigade-sized units (3,000 to 5,000 soldiers) with an NCO assistant.

LIEUTENANT GENERAL

The lieutenant general commands corps-sized units of 20,000 to 40,000 soldiers.

CAPTAIN

The captain commands company-sized units (75 to 200 soldiers) with an NCO assistant.

NON-COMMISSIONED

SERGEANT

A sergeant usually commands a squad of around ten soldiers. The sergeant supervises the privates' daily routines and sets an example for discipline, hard work and professional behaviour.

CORPORAL

The first rank of NCOs, corporals act as team leaders of the smallest army units and are responsible for soldiers' individual training and personal appearance.

PRIVATE

This is the army's lowest rank, and is given to new recruits when they start basic combat training (BCT). A private's role is simple – to follow orders!

WAR OF AGES

Small groups of trained, full-time soldiers have been around for thousands of years, but it is only in the last 400 years that countries have been able to afford full-time military protection.

Roman soldiers held shields above their heads and in front of them to form a 'shieldwall'. This wall protected them from their enemy's weapons.

ANCIENT ARMIES

The Spartans in ancient Greece were one of the earliest professional armies. At seven, young boys were sent to live in barracks to train as soldiers. They devoted their lives to the service of their country until they retired at 60 years old. Meanwhile, the Roman Army was made up of men who were required to serve for a certain number of years – an early form of conscription. In around 115 BCE, it became a professional army – made up of Roman citizens who served for 25 years before being discharged from the army.

FIGHTING FOR MONEY

In the Middle Ages, many countries couldn't afford to pay full-time armies, so they hired mercenaries. These were professional soldiers who were paid by whichever side could afford them to fight their battles during times of conflict. By the seventeenth century, most countries had permanent armies, but these were usually still trained and organised by mercenaries.

BEST OF BRITISH

The British Army was formed in 1707 when the English and Scottish armies were united. The army was well organised and very well equipped. During the eighteenth century, the British Army fought important battles against the French, Scots and the USA. The Napoleonic Wars against France caused the army to grow rapidly from 40,000 men in 1793 to 250,000 by 1813.

Unlike ancient armies, most modern armies now include women in all services.

AMERICAN INDEPENDENCE

The US Army was formed in 1775 with George Washington as its leader. Its job was to fight against the UK. In the nineteenth century, armies from the north and south of the US fought against each other in the American Civil War, and more than 600,000 soldiers were killed. Long-running battles followed with Native Americans, and a civil war against its neighbour, Mexico. All this meant that the USA was less involved with international conflicts, and joined World War I only in 1917, three years after it started.

Modern-day warfare

Following the two World Wars, the British Army was reduced in size, and often served a peacekeeping role – although there were still smaller conflicts over independence in the former British colonies of Cyprus, Kenya and Malaya. Troop numbers continue to reduce, as technology plays an increasingly important role in modern warfare. All this still comes at a price. The USA is currently responsible for 43 per cent of the world's total military spending.

THE M2 BRADLEY

The M2 Bradley Fighting Vehicle is one of the world's most successful tanks. Its main mission is to transport infantry squads to key areas. Here are some of its amazing features.

A 25-mm M242 Bushmaster chain gun fires up to 200 rounds per minute and is accurate up to 2.5 km.

A 7.62-mm medium machine gun is located to the right of the cannon. It is equipped with anti-tank missiles that are capable of destroying most tanks within a range of 3.75 km.

Two M257 smoke grenade launchers are each loaded with four smoke grenades.

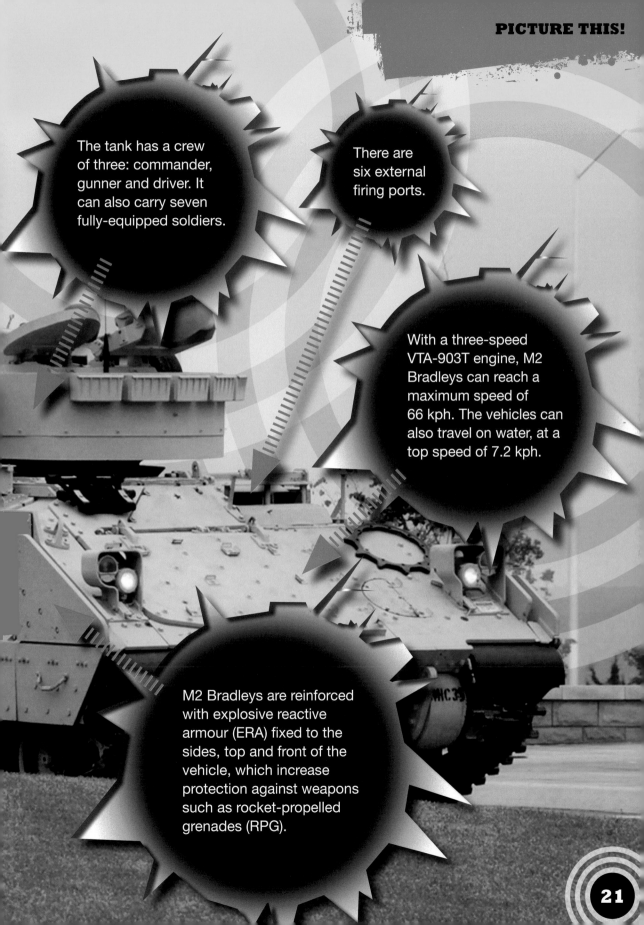

The tank has a crew of three: commander, gunner and driver. It can also carry seven fully-equipped soldiers.

There are six external firing ports.

With a three-speed VTA-903T engine, M2 Bradleys can reach a maximum speed of 66 kph. The vehicles can also travel on water, at a top speed of 7.2 kph.

M2 Bradleys are reinforced with explosive reactive armour (ERA) fixed to the sides, top and front of the vehicle, which increase protection against weapons such as rocket-propelled grenades (RPG).

THE TARZAN

The Royal Marines are a small but highly trained British naval force. Royal Marines Commando Training (RMCT) takes 32 weeks to complete, and includes time in class, on the firing range and exercises in the field. All recruits spend one week at the Marines' training centre in Devon, UK. On the fourth day, they attempt the Tarzan Assault Course.

Essential technique

- Bravery – the recruit is pushed outside of his 'comfort zone'
- Stamina – as the tests come one after the other, a recruit must stay strong to avoid making dangerous mistakes
- Balance – as the recruit moves at speed around the obstacles, if he does not stay steady, he could be seriously hurt
- Determination – a recruit needs strength of will and a true desire to succeed!

HOW IT'S DONE

1. **Commando slide** (nicknamed the Death Slide). This rapid rope descent tests the recruit's bravery, as well as his head for heights.

2. **Rope walk**. The soldier travels on hands and knees along two ropes, ten metres off the ground and shoulder-width apart, then continues across a wobbling rope bridge.

3. **Balance test**. The recruit runs across a five-metre-long wooden bar – just wide enough to place one foot in front of the other. Speed must be kept up and arms used for balance.

4. **Ten-metre rope climb**. Recruits use upper body strength to pull themselves to the top. Exhausted from the other obstacles, it looks like a mountain to climb.

WHY DO IT?

Royal Marines Commando Training is designed to produce well-drilled, combat-ready airmen and women. The Tarzan Assault Course is specifically designed to push recruits to their limits. Complete the course, and they are prepared as they will ever be for real combat conditions!

MILITARY FORCES

Radar looks at the world's biggest military spenders to see what they have got for their money.

1. THE USA

Annual military spending: £400 billion
Active troops: 1.58 million
Fighter jets: 3,000
Submarines: 71
Warships: 55

2. CHINA

Annual military spending: £59 billion
Active troops: 2.28 million
Fighter jets: 1,300
Submarines: 4
Warships: 26

3. THE UK

Annual military spending:
£41.6 billion
Active troops: 175,690
Fighter jets: 200
Submarines: 11
Warships: 23

4. FRANCE

Annual military spending:
£40.45 billion
Active troops: 352,771
Fighter jets: 300
Submarines: 10
Warships: 15

5. RUSSIA

Annual military spending:
£36.65 billion
Active troops: 1 million
Fighter jets: 1,200
Submarines: 24
Warships: 37

All figures provided are from 2009 records.

ALEX KEHOE

Petty officer Alex joined the navy when he was 18 years old, and has served for six years. Here, he tells Radar what life is like on a nuclear submarine.

What inspired you to join the navy?

My family has been going to sea for years. It's in my blood! I chose the navy over the other services to have the chance to travel the world. I was also given the opportunity to study for a degree in electrical engineering alongside my job.

How did you end up on a sub?

I started off on board ships, but I volunteered for subs. We get paid quite a lot more than 'skimmers' (sailors on normal ships), and I thought being a submariner would be far more interesting and a bit different from normal navy life.

How long do submariners spend submerged at one time?

I'm on *HMS Trenchant*, which is a Trafalgar class nuclear hunter-killer submarine. On my class of submarine, we go deep and then come back to periscope depth every few days to communicate with the UK. Other classes of submarine may go away for three months at a time and stay submerged and out of contact the entire time.

What is your job?

My main job on board is to be a Fire Control Maintainer. That means I maintain and operate the Tomahawk Land Attack Missile system, the Spearfish torpedo system and various other systems such as navigation. I haven't fired any real missiles yet but I'm sure I will one day. We are always training to keep our skills sharp because there is a lot to remember and take into account.

How many hours do you work per shift?

We work six hours on, six hours off. In your down-time you sleep, eat and shower. Most people just go to sleep when they are off, although some go on the rowing machine, lift weights or watch films. Because of the 'six-on-six-off' shift, some people will have their breakfast at the end of a watch and then go to bed.

Do you need to learn certain skills to be a submariner?

A sailor is not a submariner until he has completed his Basic Submarine Qualification (BSQ), in which you have to learn all the main systems on board. BSQ is vital so everyone on board knows exactly what is going on in the sub and how to deal with any emergencies.

Do you ever get seasick?

I have felt seasick from time to time. It really depends on how rough it is, where you are sitting on the sub (higher up is worse) and what you are doing (reading is bad, for example). The good thing about subs is that if the sea is rough, we can just dive deeper and we will be fine.

Would you recommend the navy to Radar readers?

Definitely. There is so much opportunity for you to do amazing things that you wouldn't get to do as a civilian. You make very good friends, get to travel to awesome places – and get paid to do it!

27

READY FOR ACTION

A soldier's uniform has been specially designed to meet the needs of men and women in combat. Here are some of the most important bits of kit.

headgear

shatterproof glasses

HEADGEAR

The combat helmet is made from bullet-resistant material, such as Kevlar, and has an added bulletproof 'flap' at the base of the neck. Troops often wear large, shatterproof glasses for eye protection. Digital hearing devices can block out ear-damaging bomb blasts but still allow soldiers to hear spoken commands.

SUITED AND BOOTED

Standard Army Combat Uniform (ACU) has a green and brown camouflage pattern that is designed to be used in woodland, deserts and cities. Uniforms are fire-resistant and also treated to kill mosquitoes. A 'fragmentation jacket' (or bulletproof vest) is also usually worn to protect vital organs, including the heart and kidneys, from gunshots and debris from bomb blasts. Boots are tan-coloured, and come in two weights for summer or winter conditions.

An important part of each MOLLE is the vest, with different contents depending on the soldier — ammo boxes for automatic riflemen, grenades for grenadiers.

BAGS PACKED

A soldier's rucksack is known as a MOLLE (pronounced Molly), which is short for Modular Lightweight Load-carrying Equipment. It contains specially designed a sleeping bag, to work between temperatures of +40°C and -25°C. The rucksack also holds a hydration system, which is a large two-litre water bottle.

rucksack (MOLLE)

WAR OF WORDS!

Armed services have their own language. At Radar headquarters, we have lifted the lid on the lingo to give you an insight...

Allies
the countries that fought against the Axis during World War II, including the UK, the US, France and Russia

Axis
the countries that fought against the Allies during World War II, including Germany, Italy and Japan

front line
the most advanced position occupied by an armed force in enemy territory

Apache
a type of helicopter, used by the US Army and Royal Air Force

Chinook
a type of helicopter, used by the US Army and Royal Air Force

infantry
soldiers who are specially trained to fight on foot

Armoured Reconnaissance Troop Leader
a tank commander

choppers
helicopters

Kevlar
a light, strong material used in army clothing

civilian
a person who is not in the armed services

night-sight
a device that uses special technology to allow a user to 'see in the dark'

combat training
training in the weapons and tactics used in warfare

peacekeeping
using armed forces to prevent war in a region or country

conscription
a period of military service that is required by law

rations
limited food served to military personnel

enlisted soldiers
members of the armed services who are not officers

reconnaissance
the process of obtaining information about an enemy's position

regiment

also called a brigade, three or more batallions, usually made up of forces with different specialist skills

squad

a group of around ten soldiers led by an NCO

stronghold

an area where one army has complete control, and that is easy to defend

stealth capacity

the ability to avoid being spotted by enemy radar

withdrawal of troops

the removal of troops, usually gradually, from a battle zone

reunified

reunited, or became one country again

rotor blades

the long, flat 'blades' on top of a helicopter that make it fly

This image of helicopters leaving a military ship's deck at night was taken with a night-sight device.

smoke grenades

grenades that let out smoke and are used for signalling to aircraft to mark landing zones

GLOSSARY

adrenalin

a hormone found in the human body that causes the heart to beat faster

debris

rubble or fragments of something that has been destroyed, such as a building

coalition

a group formed temporarily because of shared needs

discharged

released from military service (usually after a fixed number of years)

communist

describes a person who believes in communism. Communism is a system of government in which the state plans and controls the economy, and all goods are equally shared by the people

liberated

freed

multinational

made up of groups from several different countries

morale

happiness or positive mental state

supersonic

faster than the speed of sound

FEEL THE FORCE!

THE FORCES ONLINE

All the services have great websites, with news from around the world, career advice and articles on military history. You can even follow them on Facebook and Twitter. Here are just a few links:

British Army
www.army.mod.uk
British Navy
www.royal-navy.mod.uk
Royal Air Force
www.raf.mod.uk
US Army
www.army.mil
US Air Force
www.airforce.com
US Navy
www.navy.mil

MUSEUMS WITH YOUR MOUSE!

Get hands-on with wartime history at the British Imperial War Museum:
www.iwm.org.uk

The US Army Center of Military History has a brilliant collection of photographs and posters dating back nearly 100 years:
www.history.army.mil

APPS

Take a look at the *World War* app – choose your weapons and save your country from defeat. For details on armed services around the world, try *Armed Forces (Encyclopedia of Soldiers)*. Download them both at:
www.itunes.com

INDEX

More Radar titles coming soon!

Graffiti Culture
Street Art
Body Decoration
Cool Brands
Being a Pro Footballer
Being a DJ
Being a Stuntman

Being a Snowboarder
Being a Model
Being a Formula 1 Racing Driver
Celebrity Make-up Artist
Celebrity Fashion Stylist
Celebrity Photographer

Are you on the Radar?